T2-COZ-691

D0535666

First 1000 Words

HINKLER BOOKS

Julie Haydon

First published in 2006
by Hinkler Books Pty Ltd
45–55 Fairchild Street
Heatherton Victoria 3202 Australia
www.hinklerbooks.com

© Hinkler Books Pty Ltd 2006

10 9 8 7 6 5 4 3 2
11 10 09 08 07

Internal Design: Ivan Finnegan
Cover Design: Hinkler Design Studio
Photography: Peter Wakeman
Prepress: Graphic Print Group

All rights reserved. No part of this
publication may be reproduced, stored
in a retrieval system, or transmitted in
any way or by any means, electronic,
mechanical, photocopying, recording
or otherwise, without the prior written
permission of Hinkler Books Pty Ltd.

ISBN-10: 1 7415 7928 7
ISBN-13: 978 1 7415 7928 4

Printed and bound in China

CONTENTS

THE
Face

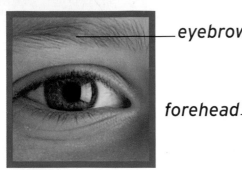

eyebrow

eye

eyelashes

eyelid

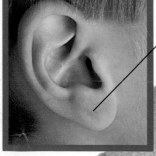

earlobe

ear

hair

forehead

mouth

lip

A HAPPY FACE

nostril

nose

tongue

teeth

tasting

touching

seeing

smelling

hearing

cheek

chin

THE
Body

head

shoulder

neck

arm

chest

abdomen

finger

wrist

waist

hip

hand

6

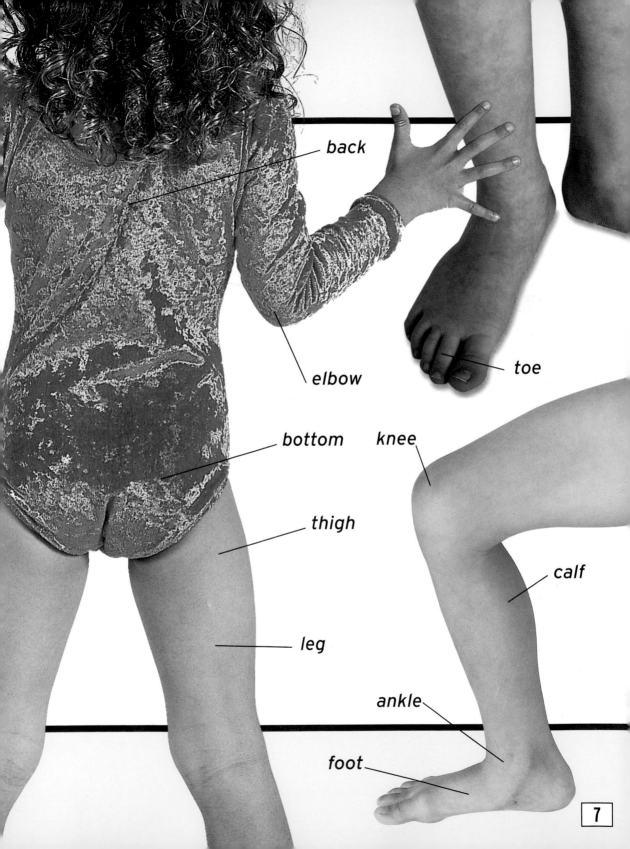

back

elbow

toe

bottom

knee

thigh

calf

leg

ankle

foot

7

MY
Family

my birth certificate

my brother

my pa

my kitten

my nana

my twin

ME

8

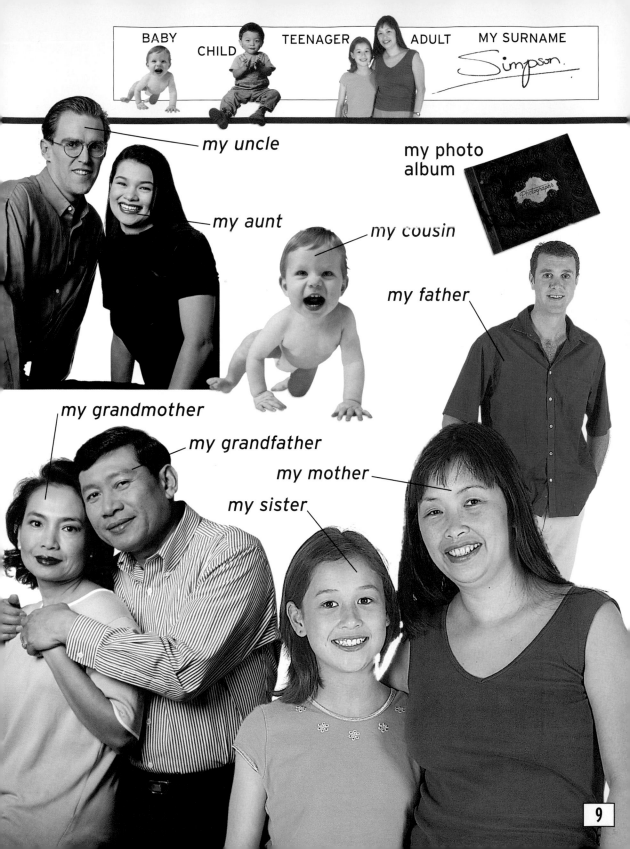

BABY
CHILD
TEENAGER
ADULT
MY SURNAME
Simpson.

my uncle

my photo album

my aunt

my cousin

my father

my grandmother

my grandfather

my mother

my sister

9

BABY'S
Things

bootees

blanket

pins

high chair

rattle

potty

cotton balls

soft toy

monitors

BIB

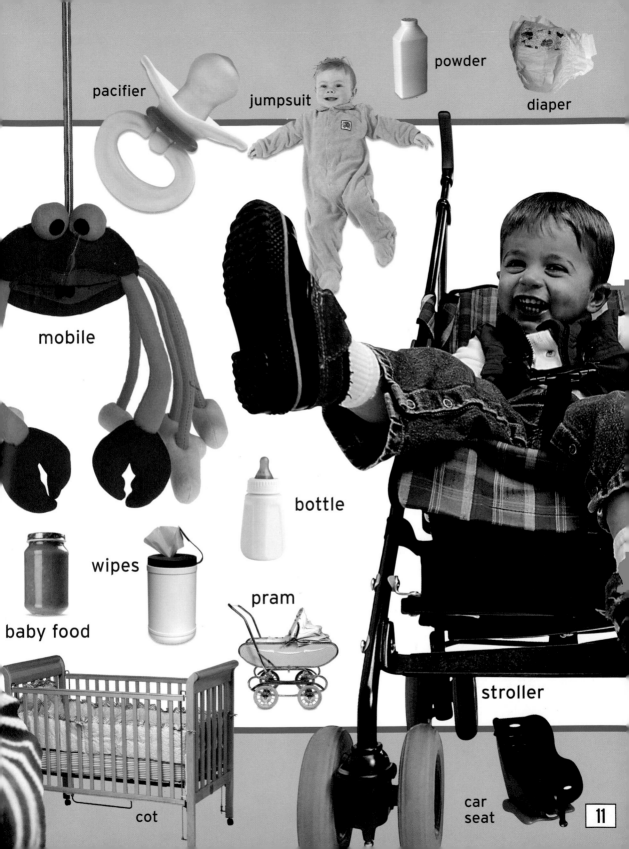

pacifier

jumpsuit

powder

diaper

mobile

bottle

wipes

baby food

pram

stroller

cot

car seat

11

Clothes

tights

shorts

sweater

overalls

jeans

singlet

BOOTS

coat

tie

trousers

underpants

shoes

T-shirt

dress

leotard

shirt

skirt

socks

underpants

jacket

sneakers

13

Accessories

satchel

hat

hairclip

key ring

beret

braces

EARRING

headband

ribbons

necklace

scrunchies

backpack

handbag

evening bag

gloves

belt

watch

cap

rings

fake tattoo

bracelets

15

Food

egg

sandwich

sugar

butter

cereal

juice

yogurt

bread

FISH

granola bars

crackers

hot chocolate

oatmeal

milk

cheese

meat

rice

pasta

honey

salad

PARTY Food

muffin

fried chicken

fruit tart

potato chips

JELLYBEANS

pies

lollipop

donut

popcorn

jello

cookies

mandarin orange

dates

strawberry

pineapple

apple

lemon

watermelon

grapes

peaches

ma

21

Vegetables

asparagus

onion

cabbages

leeks

carrots

cauliflower

SWEET CORN

radish

spinach

mushrooms

rhubarb

broccoli

zucchini

parsnip

beet

lettuce

green
onions

turnip

potatoes

eggplant

peas

23

Plants

acorns

fern

grass

holly

ivy

blossom

cactus

LEAVES

seedling

pine cone

moss

trunk

bark

bottlebrush

wattle

gum flowers

palm tree

oak leaves

weeping willow

maple

flytrap

pot plants

25

Flowers

pansy

violet

bouquet

daisy

chrysanthemum

orchid

bluebell

SUNFLOWER

tulip

cornflower

knotweed

gardenia

26

zinnia

carnation

hibiscus

marigold

iris

rose

lily

freesia

gerbera

Gardening

trowel

potting mix

gardening gloves

shears

faucet

spade

SHED

hose

bulbs

watering can

seeds

compost bin

flowerpots

clippers

gardening hat

wheelbarrow

lawnmower

rake

shovel

weeds

rock

LARGE Mammals

cheetah

tiger

lion

elephant

bear

WHALE

hippopotamus

sea lion

rhinoceros

polar bear

deer

monkey

dolphins

kangaroo

camel

leopard

giraffe

chimpanzee

puma

gorilla

moose

SMALL Mammals

hedgehog

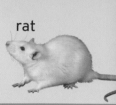

rat

squirrel

otter

raccoon

meerkats

BADGER

koala

opossum

fox

echidna

skunk

wombat

chipmunk

hare

possum

wolverine

bat

beaver

Tasmanian devil

armadillo

Birds

emu

pigeon

owl

kingfisher

puffin

parrot

ALBATROSS

eagle

macaw

pelican

ostrich

falcon

hawk

lovebird

flamingo

crane

peacock

toucan

swans

vulture

woodpecker

REPTILES AND
Amphibians

bullfrog

alligator

skink

iguana

gecko

KOMODO DRAGON

cobra

terrapin

tortoise

toad

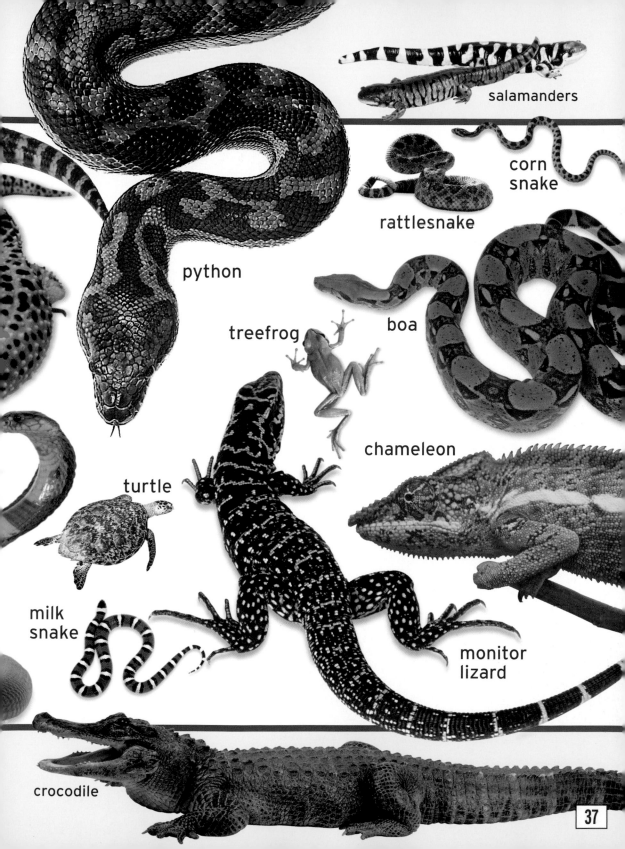

salamanders

corn snake

rattlesnake

python

boa

treefrog

chameleon

turtle

milk snake

monitor lizard

crocodile

37

WATER
Animals

puffer fish

lobster

herrings

tuna

oysters

prawn

JELLYFISH

angelfish

stingray

seadragon

coral

shark

damsel fish

cod

sardines

salmon

sea horse

starfish

catfish

crab

eel

pike

Mini-beasts

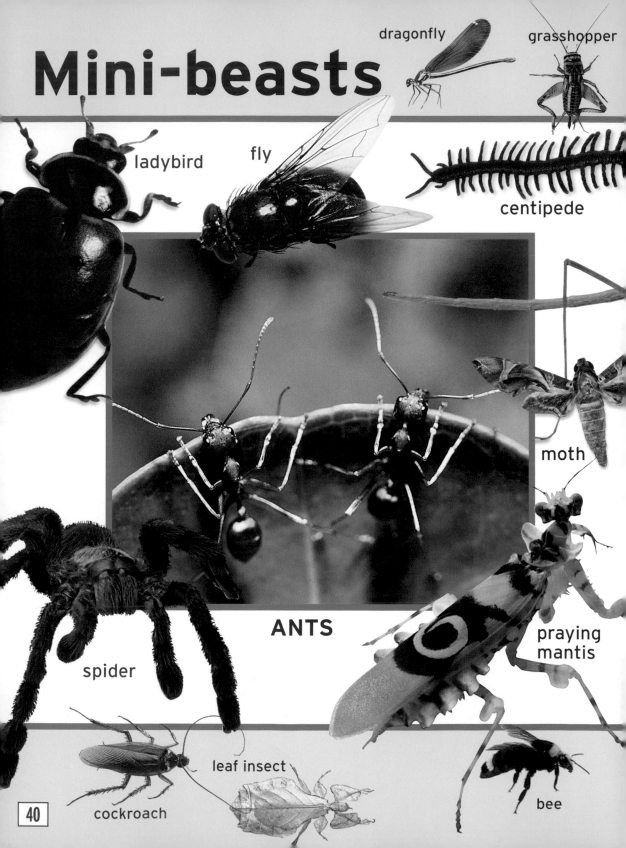

dragonfly

grasshopper

ladybird

fly

centipede

moth

ANTS

praying mantis

spider

cockroach

leaf insect

bee

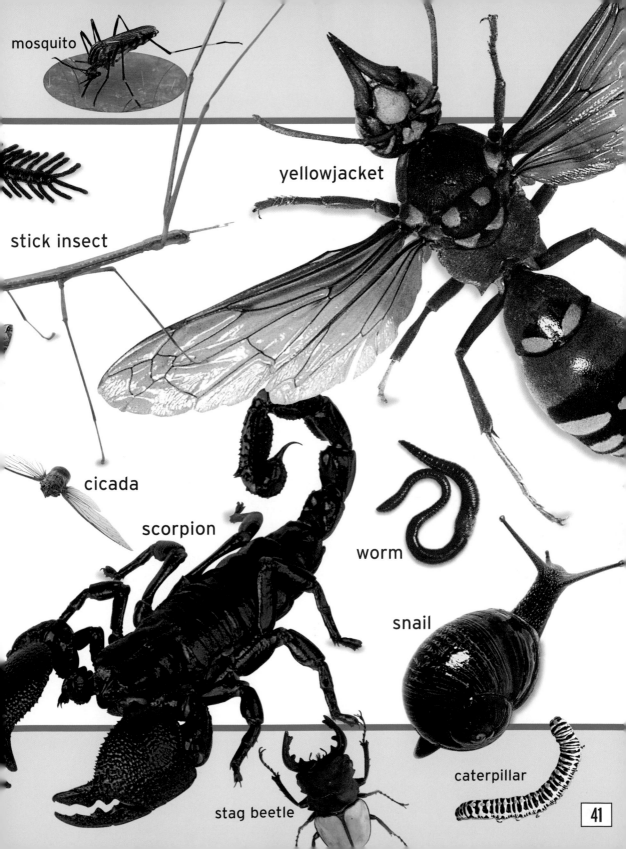

mosquito

yellowjacket

stick insect

cicada

scorpion

worm

snail

stag beetle

caterpillar

41

ANIMAL Bodies

hoof

feathers

horn

wings

FANGS

tail

fur

spines

talons

whiskers

42

gill

scales

paw

claws

mane

snout

antlers

pouch

tusks

beak

fin

Pets

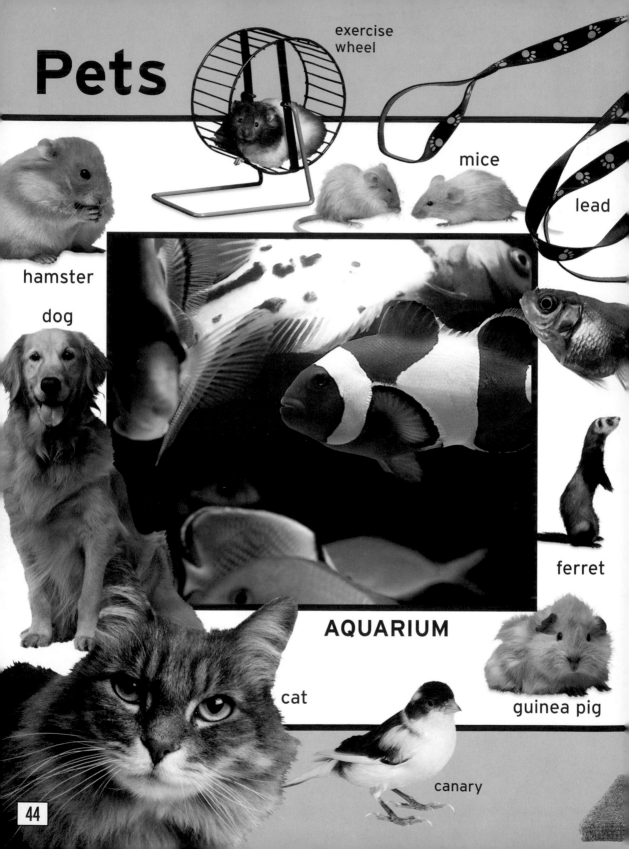

exercise wheel

mice

lead

hamster

dog

ferret

AQUARIUM

guinea pig

cat

canary

pony

kennel

collar

tug toy

rabbit

goldfish

cage

stable

saddle

scratching post

pet bed

A House

door knocker

mailbox

balcony

window

curtain

lawn

doormat

lock

wall

blind

door

porch

gutter

fence

bricks

garage

drive

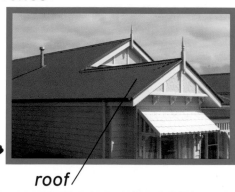

roof

trash can

doorknob

IN THE
Bedroom

chest of drawers

night-light

photo frame

quilt

pillow

alarm clock

toy box

trophy

BED

books

The Folk of the Faraway Tree

dressing gown

wardrobe

slippers

hobby horse

pajamas

mattress

hat tree

teddy bear

rug

poster

IN THE
Bathroom

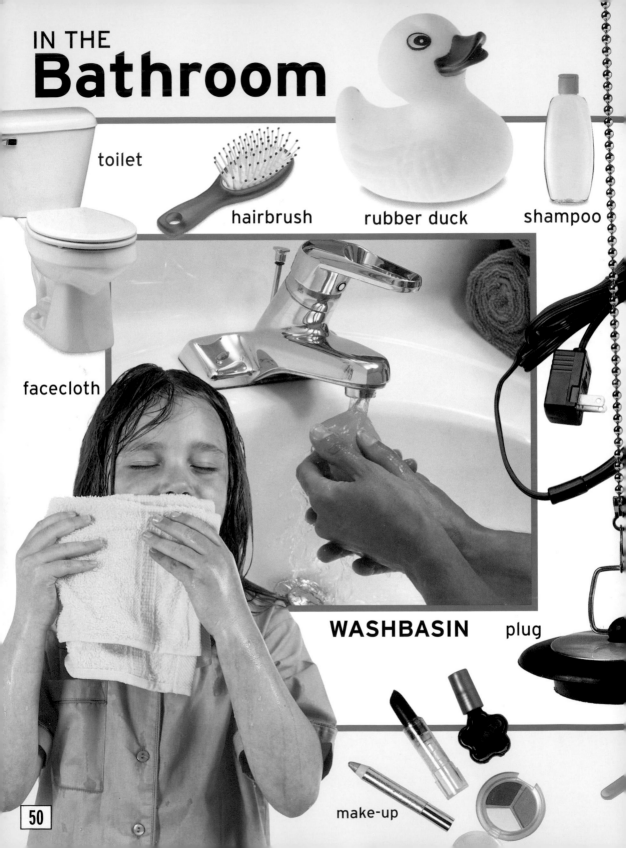

toilet

hairbrush

rubber duck

shampoo

facecloth

WASHBASIN

plug

make-up

medicine

tissues

comb

toothpaste

toilet paper

shower

hairdryer

mirror

towel

bath

toothbrush

soap

bubble bath

51

IN THE
Family Room

video recorder

coffee table

lamp

remote control

rocking chair

cushion

BOOKSHELF

vase

television

compact disc

video cassettes

picture

carpet

beanbag

games table

coasters

headphones

sofa

newspaper

stereo

magazines

53

IN THE
Kitchen

juicer

kitchen scales

electric mixer

oven

cooktop

apron

toaster

stool

BENCHTOP

refrigerator

food processor

54

table

breadboard

chair

jar

breadmaker

kettle

cookbook

sink

dishwasher

microwave oven

IN THE
Cupboard

bowl

saucepan

cake tin

plate

detergent

PLATTER

sponge

teapot

cup

dishtowel

rubber gloves

rolling pin

wooden
spoon

glass

knife

fork

spoon

tray

egg beater

fry pan

jug

57

IN THE
Study

envelope

desk

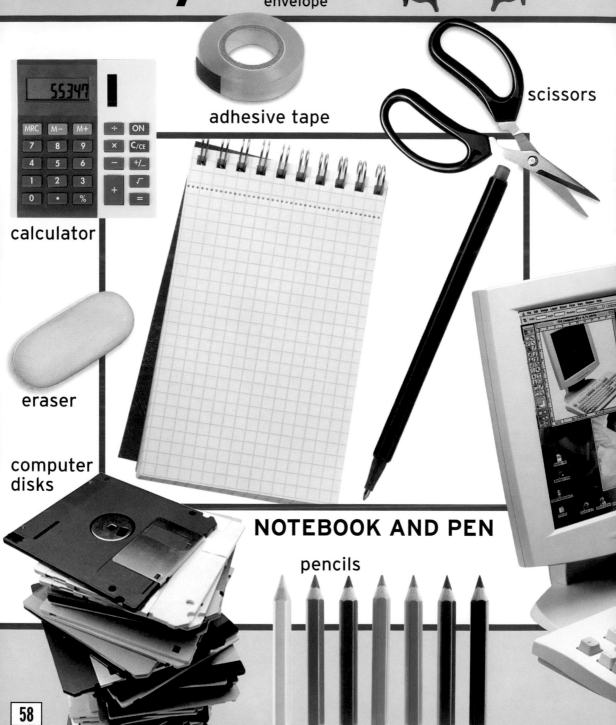

adhesive tape

scissors

calculator

eraser

computer
disks

NOTEBOOK AND PEN

pencils

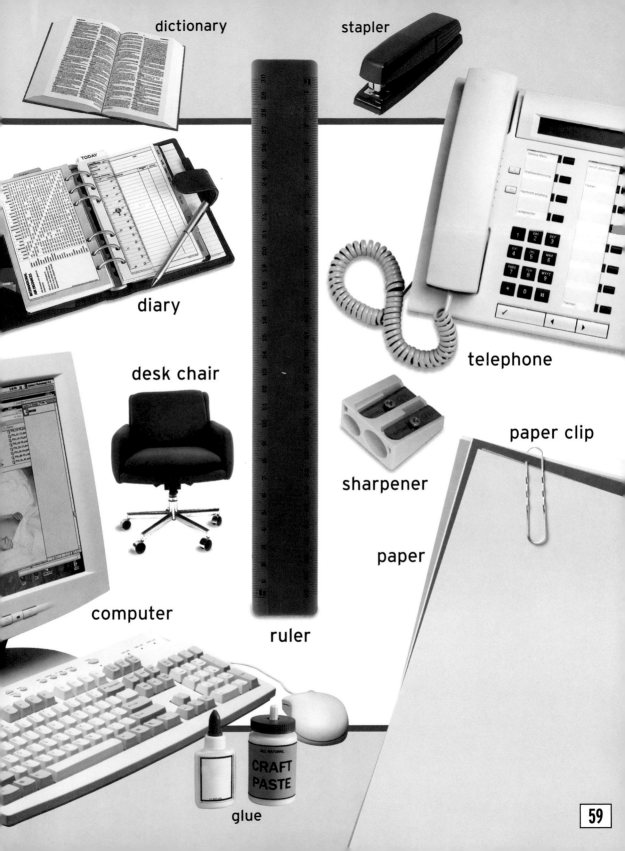

dictionary

stapler

diary

telephone

desk chair

sharpener

paper clip

paper

computer

ruler

glue

HOUSEHOLD
Items

nails

pliers

screw

power point

ax

coat-hanger

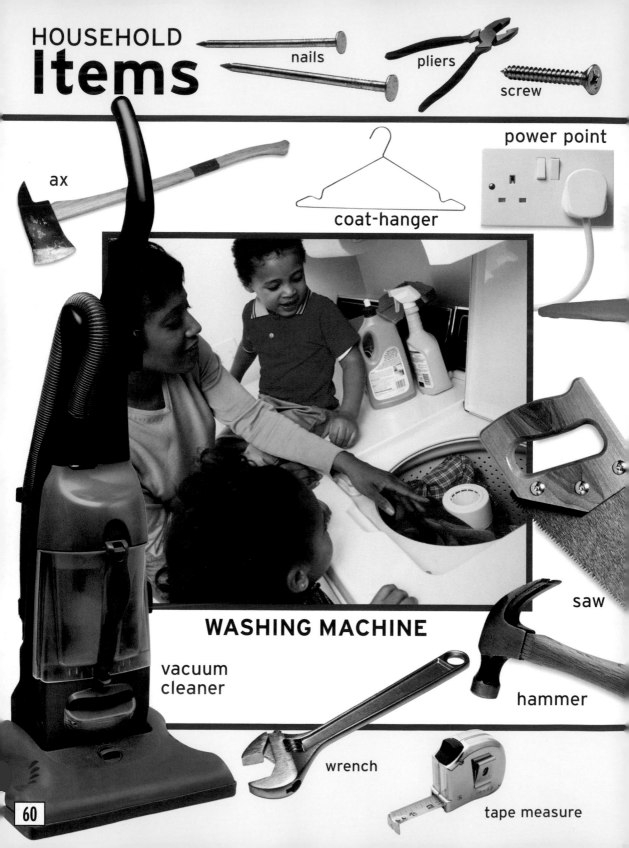

WASHING MACHINE

saw

vacuum cleaner

hammer

wrench

tape measure

paintbrush

screwdrivers

iron

dryer

ladder

ironing board

tool kit

paint tin

electric drill

Birthday Party

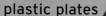

plastic plates

candy

banner

birthday card

plastic cup

BIRTHDAY CAKE

wrapping paper

presents

candles

take-home bag

streamers

fruit drink

bow

party whistles

invitation

straws

badge

paper hat

birthday girl

mask

friends

party game

63

Fancy Dress

wand

bumblebee

glitter

Little
Bo Peep

king

butterfly

mouse

octopus

flower

64

puss

tiara

fairy wings

sea lion

costume

bunny

starfish

puppy

calf

pirate

wig

clown

Toys

dice

doll's house

dinosaur

wagon

soldier

dragon

blackboard

PUZZLE

cowboy

checkerboard

cube

skipping rope

doll

cards

spaceship

robot

tricycle

blocks

slinky

dominoes

marbles

67

FAVORITE Things

jewelry

kite

boomerang

money

crayons

piggy bank

penguin

SEE-SAW

telescope

ukulele

stickers

scarf

magnet

quilt

fishing rod

chess set

coconut

Frisbee

tutu

radio

yo-yo

69

SPORTS Equipment

basketball

rollerblades

baseball glove

bicycle helmet

cricket bat

dartboard

sailboard

SURFBOARD

soccer ba[ll]

flippers

baseball bat

ice skates

whistle

skis

stopwatch

darts

bicycle

goggles

wetsuit

tennis racket

football

hockey stick

MUSICAL Instruments

bells

flute

clarinet

triangle

harp

ACOUSTIC GUITAR

cello

maracas

xylophone

piano

recorder

accordion

banjo

tambourine

trumpet

cymbals

saxophone

bagpipes

drums

electric
guitar

violin

ON THE
Farm

scarecrow

horse

foal

chick

hen

pig

donkey

duck

SHEEPDOG

lamb

rooster

tractor

cow

farmer

farmhouse

goats

sheep

field

goose

hay bale

gate

75

AT THE
Beach

ice cream

beach ball

deckchair

seaweed

sunscreen

ROCK POOL

swim ring

shells

sea

bucket
and
spade

sandcastle

beach
umbrella

sand

seagull

sailboat

swimsuit

sunhat

drink

sandals

basket

sunglasses

Camping

hiking boot

camp bed

trail mix

Swiss army knife

binoculars

thermos

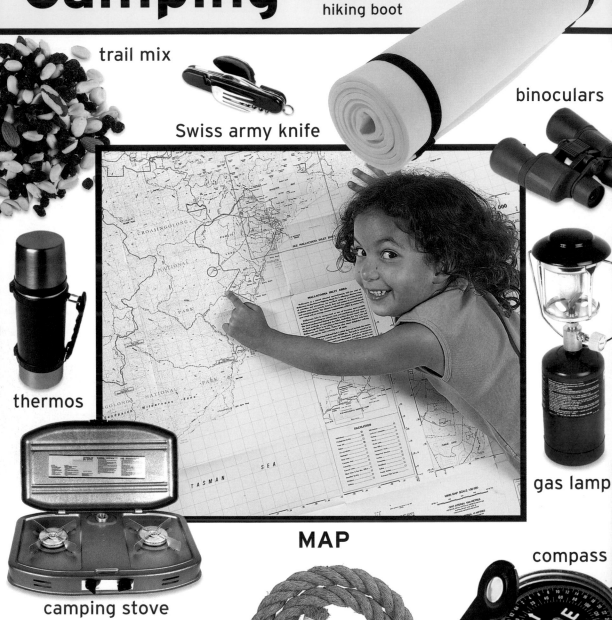

MAP

gas lamp

camping stove

compass

matches

rope

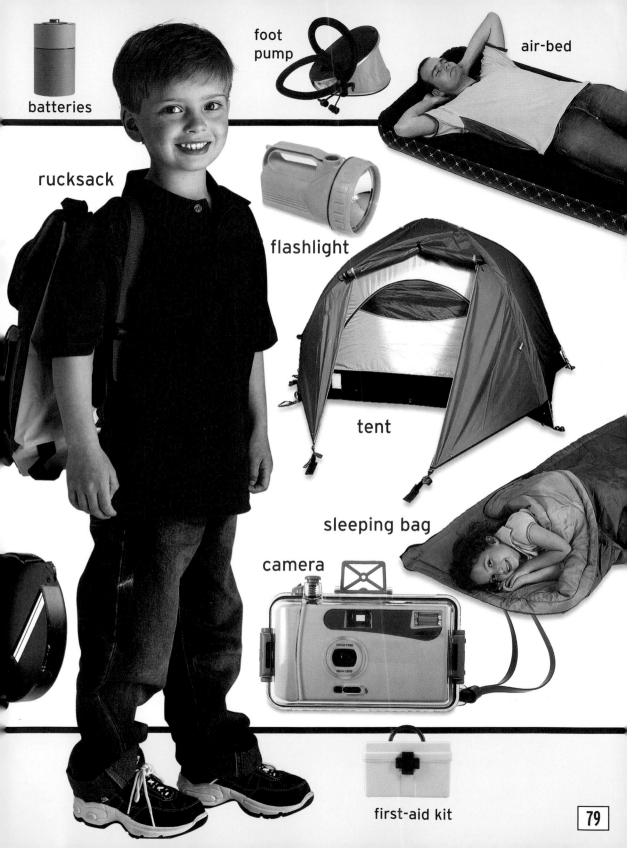

batteries

foot
pump

air-bed

rucksack

flashlight

tent

sleeping bag

camera

first-aid kit

Transport

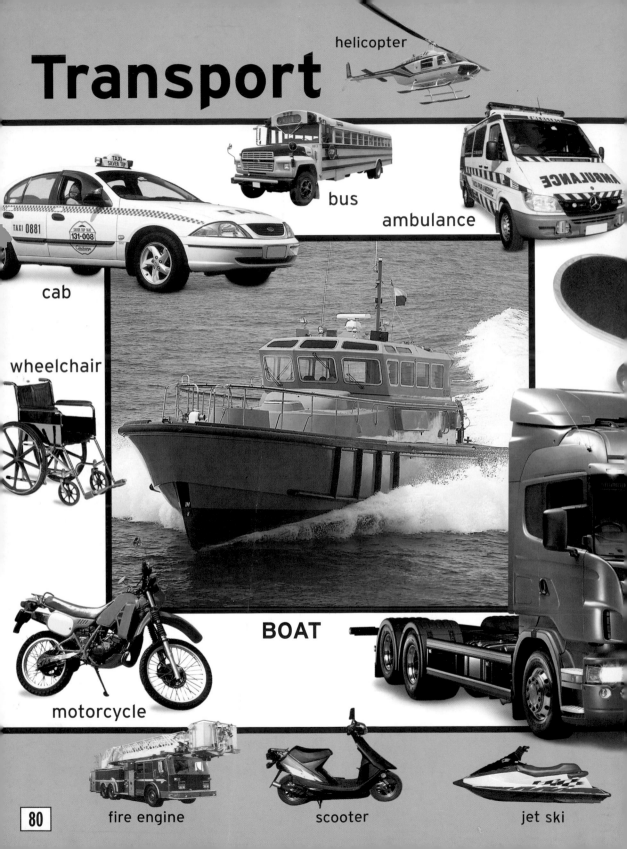

helicopter

bus

ambulance

cab

wheelchair

BOAT

motorcycle

fire engine

scooter

jet ski

judge

soccer player

plumber

police officer

boxer

waiter

astronaut

nurse

builder

office worker

teacher

Actions

walking

climbing

drawing

talking

hugging

sitting

HIDING

crying

reading

drinking

sleeping

running

playing

cutting

eating

kicking

frowning

jumping

reaching

writing

laughing

Opposites

fat

dry

thin

wet

under

over

push

pull

86

down

up

young

old

short

long

empty

full

big

clean

small

dirty

Numbers

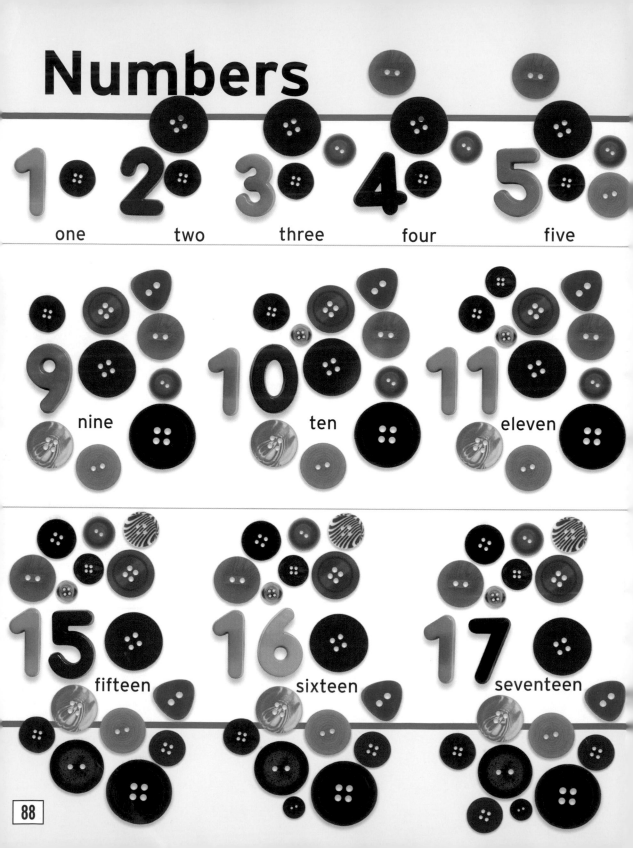

1 one

2 two

3 three

4 four

5 five

9 nine

10 ten

11 eleven

15 fifteen

16 sixteen

17 seventeen

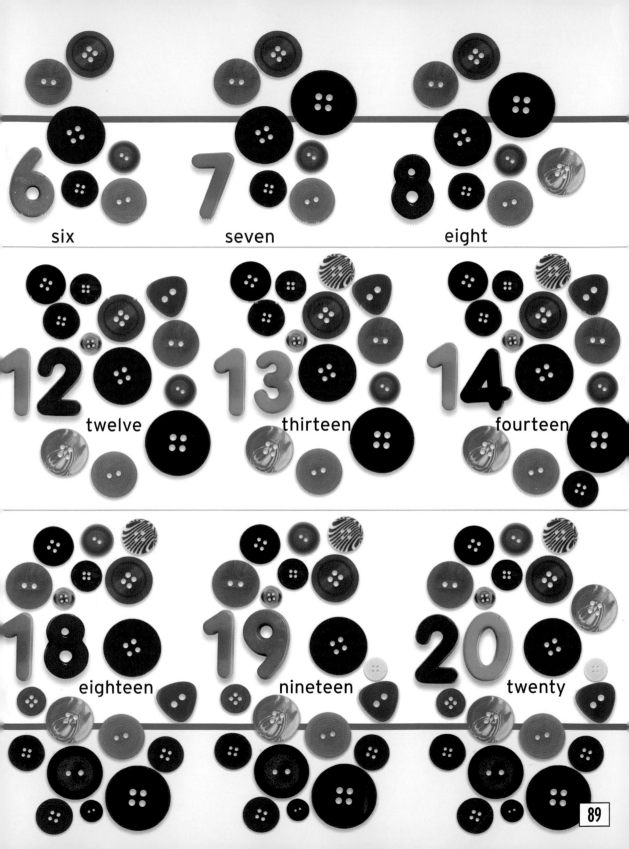

six

seven

eight

twelve

thirteen

fourteen

eighteen

nineteen

twenty

COLORS
and Shapes

green

yellow

blue

gray

orange

purple

white

red

brown

pink

black

hexagon

crescent

triangle

square

rectangle

circle

heart

diamond

STOP

octagon

star

oval

Flags

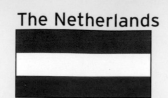

Belgium

Mexcio

Philippines

Australia

Singapore

Hungary

The Czech Republic

Norway

Poland

South Korea

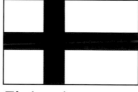
Finland

United Kingdom

Egypt

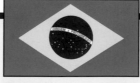
Brazil

South Africa

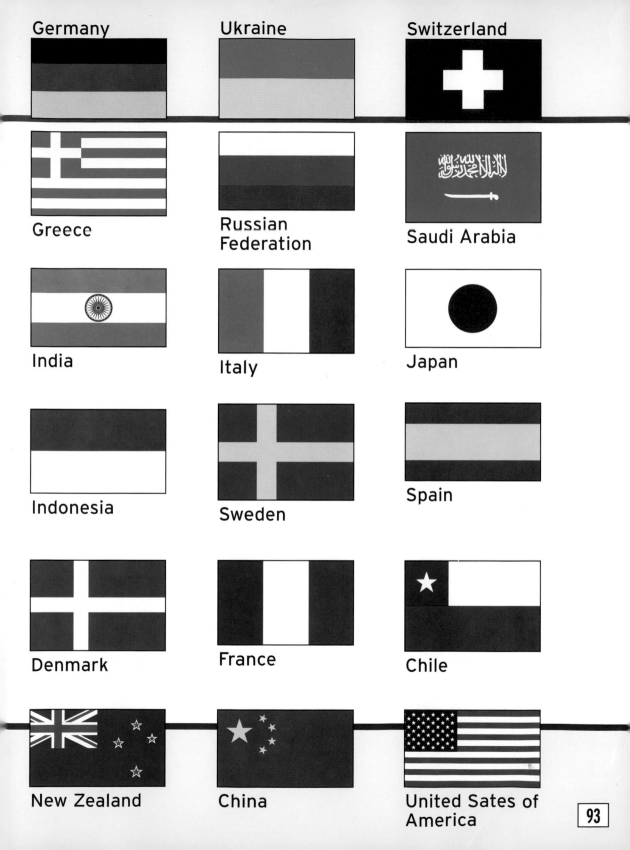

Germany

Ukraine

Switzerland

Greece

Russian Federation

Saudi Arabia

India

Italy

Japan

Indonesia

Sweden

Spain

Denmark

France

Chile

New Zealand

China

United Sates of America

93

THE
Earth and Sky

clouds

Earth

forest

MOUNTAIN

wind

lightning

desert

eclipse

rain

iceberg

river

moon

pond

rainbow

stars

storm

sun

volcano

cave

waterfall

pasture

95